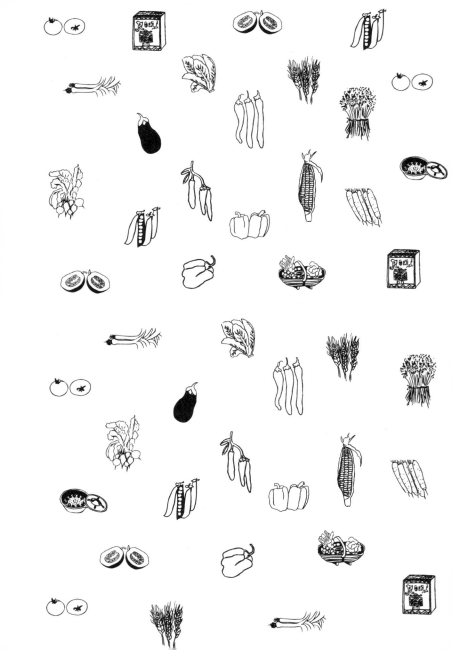

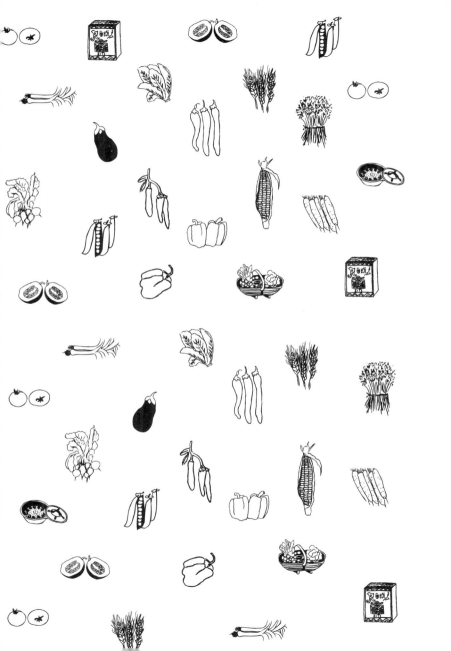

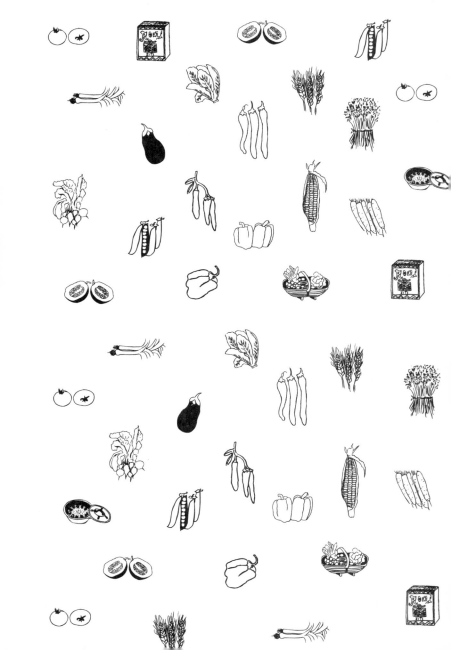

good & cheap

vegetarian dining

in New York

good & cheap

vegetarian dining

in New York

With illustrations by Susan Colgan

Arthur S. Brown & Barbara Holmes

city & company / new york

City and Company
22 W. 23rd St.
New York, NY 10010

Printed in the United States of America

Design by Iris Weinstein

Library of Congress Cataloging-in-Publication Data
is available upon request

ISBN 1-885492-26-X

First Edition

contents

Introduction   xv
Abyssinia   3
American Cafe   4
Anand Bhavan   4
Angelica Kitchen   6
Annam Brahma   7
Apple Restaurant   8
B & H Dairy   9
Bachué   9
Bamboo Garden Restaurant   10
Bell Cafe   11
Benny's Burritos   12

Blanche's Organic Cafe   12
Boostan   13
Burritoville   14
Cafe Kapulsky   15
Cafe Natural   15
Cafe Viva   16
Candle Cafe   17
Caravan of Dreams   18
Chutney Mary   18
Commodities Coffee Bar   19
Dairy Palace   20
Diamond Dairy   20
Dining at Rubi's   21
Doctor Squeeze   22
Dojo   22
Eden Rock   23
Eva's   24
Everything Natural   24
Everything Vital   25
Famous Pita   26
Freddie and Pepper's
 Gourmet Pizzeria   27
Good Food Cafe   27
Good Health Cafe   28
Gourmet Cafe   29
Govinda's   29
Great American Health Bar   30

x

**Gulliver's Living and Learning Center—
Liliput Cafe   30**
Hangawi   31
Health Pub   32
Healthy Chelsea   32
Healthy Henrrieta's   33
Healthy Pleasures   34
Helianthus   34
Hong Kong Vegetarian   35
House of Falafel   36
House of Vegetarian   36
Hunan Delight   37
Indian Delhi   38
Integral Yoga   39
I Rankin' Ital Stop   39
Josephina   40
Josie's   41
Kar   41
Kar Luk   42
Kinish Nosh   43
Kosher Corner   43
Le Poeme   44
Lenox Ave. Health Food Restaurant   44
Life Cafe   45
Liveth's Delight Vegetarian Restaurant   46
Lucky's Juice Joint   46
Madras Mahal   47

Mana 48

Matamim Kosher Dairy Restaurant 48

Mathilda's Bakery, M...M...M... 49

Mavali Palace 50

Melanie's Natural Cafe 51

Michael & Zoë's 51

Mr. Falafel 52

Mrs. Stahl's Knishes 53

Natural Food Bar 53

Nature Works 54

Nyota's Ting 55

Oasis 55

Ozu 56

Planet One 57

Plum Tree 58

Quantum Leap 58

Ratner's Dairy Restaurant 59

Red Hot Szechuan 60

Salad Bowl 60

Salad Daze 61

Sanctuary 62

Smile of the Beyond 62

Souen 63

Spring Street Natural 64

**Steve & Sons Bakery,
  Restaurant & Caterers** 64

Strictly Roots 65

Taqueria 66
Temple in the Village 66
Teva Natural Foods 67
Topaz 68
Uptown Juice Bar and Vegetarian Deli 68
Vegetable Garden 69
Vege Vege II 70
Vegetarian Delights 71
Vegetarian Garden 71
Vegetarian Heaven 72
Vegetarian Paradise 73
Village Natural 74
Weiss' Kosher Dairy Restaurant 75
West Indian Vegetarian
  and Seafood Restaurant 75
Whole Earth Bakery and Kitchen 76
Whole Foods in SoHo 77
Who's on Seventh? 77
Yonah Shimmel's 78
Zen Palate 78
Glossary 81
Index by Neighborhood 85
Index by Cuisine 93

introduction

Welcome to *Good & Cheap Vegetarian Dining in New York*, formerly published under the title *Vegetarian Dining in New York City (and not just the places the yuppies like)* and updated since 1991. For all our old fans, this book will serve as the fifth edition. We're grateful for your continuing support. To all our new readers, thank you for selecting our guide.

My own commitment to vegetarianism began in my 20s, when I realized that a meat-centered diet was affecting my health. I also began to reawaken my awareness of the waste of resources, negative impact on our environment, and suffering that a meat-centered diet creates. To my mind, all good reasons. One of the best reasons I ever heard, though, was expressed by the novelist Isaac Bashevis Singer, who, in answer to the question, "Do you avoid eating meat for your health?" replied: "No, for the animal's health." Increasing numbers of people are cutting back on the consumption of meat for reasons of personal health, concern for the environment, spirituality, and the love of animals, to mention just a few. Even our government, in the form of the USDA, is urging us to cut back.

As a native New Yorker, I know New York. I love to walk around the city's neighborhoods and drop into new restaurants that offer vegetarian menus. Barbara, a dietician, has a lifelong interest in the connection between food and health, and our daughter Jasmine shares with us her unique perspective. The three of us dine out constantly, and so we began to keep a list of where to get good vegetarian meals, noting our opinions of each. As our list grew, and became more comprehensive, we realized that it might be useful to others.

Included in this guide are only those restaurants that are either completely vegetarian or that offer a substantial number of vegetarian entrees. The choice of restaurants represents the subjective tastes of the authors. In addition, we've included some places that also serve meat, in order to provide the greatest number of options, and to accommodate anyone dining out with others who are not strictly vegetarian. Since New York restaurants often come and go, it's always best to call first.

We hope you find our guide helpful. We've tried to make it as thorough and easy to use as possible, but if we've omitted your favorite restaurant, or if you have any comments, please drop us a line; your feedback will help us to improve future editions. You can also write to us for a free update of recent restaurant openings and closings. Simply send a stamped, self-addressed envelope to: Vegetarian Dining, City & Company, 22 W. 23 St., New York, New York 10010. Our Internet address is Vegmaven@aol.com.

key to prices

We've broken down price into four basic categories: inexpensive, moderate, moderate-expensive, and expensive. Since a primary focus of our book is to promote low-cost dining, our parameters are lower than those of other guides.

For the average price of an entree without any extras (i.e., dessert or alcohol):

Inexpensive: $6 and under
Moderate: $6–$9
Moderate-Expensive: $9–$12
Expensive: $12 and over

good & cheap

vegetarian dining

in New York

abyssinia

35 Grand St. between Sixth Ave. and W. Broadway • 226–5959
Hours: Monday through Friday 6 pm to 11 pm

If you've never eaten authentic Ethiopian food, now is the time. You sit around a large wicker table in the center of which is placed a large tray of Injera (a crepe-like flatbread). Your food is served on top of this "bread." To eat, tear off pieces of the Injera and sop up your food with it. Some vegetarian items include azefa wot (a lentil dish with onions and ginger), shuro (a delicious puree of chickpeas, garlic, and tomatoes) and yegomen wot (kale and potatoes sauteed with onions, green peppers and spices). Small children will love it here, because Ethiopian food traditionally is eaten with the hands. Sooner or later, somebody drinks too much honey wine and falls off their three-legged chair. Great fun, educational, and a large selection of delicious vegetarian dishes.

Moderate

american cafe

160 Broadway near Maiden Lane • 732–1426
Hours: Monday through Thursday 7 am to 8 pm; Friday 7 am to 3 pm;
Closed Saturday and Sunday

A great little kosher dairy restaurant in the heart of the financial district. For those who don't know, to be certified kosher (a strictly observed process), an establishment or kitchen must exclude any and all animal products (except milk, eggs, and certain types of fish). Great news if you're a lacto–ovo vegetarian, so-so news if you're a vegan. Veggie burgers are made with vegetables and beans and served on seven–grain English muffins; vegetable chili is served over brown rice, and much more (including some great Israeli staples like humous, babaganoush and falafel).

Inexpensive

anand bhavan

35–66 73rd St. near Roosevelt Ave.
Jackson Heights, Queens • 718-507–1600
Hours: Daily Noon to 9:30 pm

Located in the Jackson Heights area known as "Little India," this restaurant, formerly called Udupi Palace, offers good, cheap vegetarian Indian vittles, in the great Hindu and Jain

4

tradition. Most dishes are under $6, except for the curries, which are mostly $6.25. Full dinners (six courses and up) range from $11 to $13. The lunch special is a particularly good deal. Some goodies include the medhu vada (fried lentil doughnuts), which are simply scrumptious. Dip them in a delicious chutney made with coconut and cilantro. The gobi masala curry (cauliflower and spices), the kancheepurum iddly (lentil patties with cashews, ginger, and coriander), and the coconut uthappam are all superb as well. If you frequent South Indian restaurants, you know that "thali" means a platter with rice and papadam (crispy bread) in the middle, surrounded by various small dishes. This is a nice combination of various tastes, from the very hot rasam, a traditional South Indian-style soup, to cool raita, a traditional yogurt-based condiment designed to cool off your tongue. The masala dosai is very impressive—huge crepes filled with potatoes, onions, carrots, and nuts. The badam halwa (ground almonds cooked in honey and butter) for dessert is wonderful.

Moderate

angelica kitchen

300 E. 12th St. between First and Second Aves. • 228–2909
Hours: Daily 11:30 am to 10:30 pm

Strictly vegan, mostly macrobiotic, quite ascetic restaurant with a vast and impeccable menu. Formerly on St. Marks Pl. near Second Ave., the space on 12th St. is light and airy, like a macrobiotic eclair. OK, here's what you do—have a seat at the communal table next to all the other serious people—careful, don't smile or express anything resembling joy or abandon. Next, order some really good, conscientiously prepared food. If you feel like an appetizer you might try one of the following: freshly baked corn bread with tahini spread or carrot butter, homemade sauerkraut, or the vegetable paté, all delectable. For your entree, try the Dragon Bowl, assorted vegetables, beans, rice, seaweed, salad, etc., served in a beautiful bowl with a picture of a dragon at the bottom. The soba with tahini sauce is great too (just a touch of horseradish). After your meal, try a calming glass of Mu Tea – a macrobiotic staple. All told, in spite of the serious atmosphere, Angelica's has long been, and still is, the NYC model for delicious, healthy food.

Moderate

 6

annam brahma

84–43 164th St. at 85th Ave.

Jamaica, Queens • 718–523–2600

Hours: Monday, Tuesday, and Thursday through Saturday 11 am to 10 pm; Wednesday 11 am to 2 pm; Sunday Noon to 10 pm

Call first to ensure that they're open, as the hours fluctuate.

Inexpensive vegetarian food served and prepared in an inspiring atmosphere by disciples of Sri Chinmoy (the weightlifting guru himself—check out the pictures of him lifting cars and stuff). They have a large menu that changes daily. Chinese dishes are prepared on Tuesdays, Italian food on Thursdays, and so on, throughout the week. Indian food is served daily. We had a fantastic dinner here one Thanksgiving that included unturkey, sweet potatoes, chestnut stuffing, cider and dessert. They do a special Christmas/New Year's feast as well. Free meditation classes are offered in the evenings and on weekends. Sri Chinmoy's books and thoughts are everywhere, and they even have a dais all set up and waiting for him in case he wanders in for coffee.

Inexpensive

apple restaurant

17 Waverly Pl. between Greene and Mercer Sts. • 473–8888
Hours: Monday through Thursday 11 am to 11 pm; Friday and
Saturday 11 am to Midnight; Sunday 11 am to 10 pm

Owned by the former proprietor of Village Natural, this
restaurant has something for everyone. Housed in what was
once a fancy French restaurant, it has a lavish interior. Its
prices, however, belie the elegance of its decor. The owners
show old movies on a little screen, offer a full bar, play excellent jazz music over the sound system, and feature
Karaoke (Japanese sing–along) as well. Although they do
have a Vietnamese meat section on their menu, they have a
huge vegetarian section also. All of the vegetarian dishes
are prepared in a separate kitchen, and most are available
without dairy. Try the crispy seitan and pecans over spinach
noodles—it's delish. A great place to have both delectable
vegetarian food and a good time.

Moderate–Expensive

b & h dairy

127 Second Ave. near 8th St. • 505–8065
Hours: Daily 7:30 am to 10 pm

A "kosher style" (their description) dairy restaurant. Good food, low prices. No meat. A gathering place for characters. They have superb, freshly baked challah bread, homemade blintzes, vegetable lasagna, and more. Specials change daily. Besides, how many other dairy restaurants can you go to on Saturday? If you're claustrophobic, though, this is probably *not* the best place for you, as it's really tiny. Pay strict attention, or you'll be eating your neighbor's food by mistake.

Inexpensive

bachué

36 W. 21st St. between Fifth and Sixth Aves. • 229–0870
Hours: Monday and Tuesday 8 am to 6 pm: Wednesday through Friday 8 am to 10 pm; Saturday 10 am to 10 pm; closed Sunday

A totally vegan, well-planned menu with the focus on South American cuisine, Bachué (pronounced bah–chew–way) is a goddess of Colombia's Chibcha people. It's also one of the best places in New York to experience gourmet vegan cuisine. Inspired by the ideas of Anne Marie Colbin from the

Natural Gourmet Cookery School (which you can reach at 645-5170), they also have a home-delivery service called "Earth Cuisine." When last there, we had the seitan with mushroom-scallion glaze, which was spectacular, and the stuffed cabbage with grilled tofu and onion gravy, which was fantastic. Bachué uses many organic ingredients, and none of the dishes include any meat, dairy products, eggs, or honey. They also serve a number of scrumptious vegan breakfasts all day long.

Inexpensive

bamboo garden restaurant

41–28 Main St. near 41st Rd.
Flushing, Queens • 718–463–9240
Hours: Daily 11 am to 10:30 pm

Vegetarian Chinese restaurant in the heart of Flushing right near the subways, buses, and general hubbub. Sister restaurant of the very wonderful Vegetarian Heaven on Manhattan's Columbus Circle. This place has no meat, fish, dairy, MSG, or bad karma, man. Instead, they boast 116 varieties of mock chicken, fish, and meat dishes with eight different sauces. The "duck" soup is good, as are the sesame "chicken," which our daughter loved, and the shredded "pork" with mustard greens. Bamboo Garden is kosher as well. The main entrance is down a number of stairs, which would make it prohibitive for anyone in a wheelchair, but the side entrance on 41st Rd. has only two steps.

Moderate

bell cafe

310 Spring St. between Greenwich and Hudson Sts. • 334–BELL
Hours: Sunday through Thursday 11:30 pm to 2 am; Friday and Saturday 11:30 pm to 4 am

Hip and happenin' hangout with poetry on the walls, makeshift chairs and tables, and a crowd that's up-to-the-minute cool. They have a good selection of veggie offerings: vegetarian Shepherd's Pie (leeks, turnips, carrots, bean pilaf topped with horseradish cream), non–dairy pizza, tempeh loaf and quesadillas, to name just a few! Monthly "art parties" the first Monday of every month. This place is a cool scene, a great place to hang out late, and they're *definitely* accommodating to vegans.

Moderate

benny's burritos

113 Greenwich Ave. near Jane St., West Village • 727–0584
93 Ave. A near 6th St., East Village • 254–2054
Hours: Sunday through Wednesday 11 am to Noon; Thursday
through Saturday 11 am to 1 am

A friend of ours from San Francisco says this place is the
Real McCoy. Mexican, delicious, and cheap, and the quality is excellent. Non-dairy whole-wheat veggie burritos are
available. There's often a line to get in at both locations. The
East Village location has a take-out division right next door,
and the West Village location has a take-out division across
the street.

Moderate

blanche's organic cafe

66 E. 44th St. near Madison Ave. • 599–3445
972 Lexington Ave. near 71st St. • 717–1923
Hours: Monday through Friday 7:30 am to 6:30 pm; Saturday
9:30 am to 5:30 pm; closed Sunday

Vegan, organic, and delicious! What a combination! A
huge and extremely healthy menu. Every day holds a different selection of soups (wild mushroom, miso sea vegetable),
salads (Blanche's mesclun salad, couscous salad with veg-

etables and dried fruit), sandwiches (white bean, sundried tomato, and arugula on whole-wheat bread) and desserts (organic cookies, tarts, kantens). Excellent choice when in the Midtown East or Hunter College area.

Moderate

boostan

5 MacDougal St. near Bleecker St. • 533–9561
Hours: Monday through Friday Noon to 1 am; Saturday and Sunday Noon to 2 am

Mediterranean vegetarian restaurant serving pasta, steamed veggies, some dairy and fish dishes, as well as a variety of things in a pita. The vegetarian moussaka is very good indeed, as are the eggplant sandwich and the potato–mushroom pie. The humous-stuffed avocado is an innovative idea, and the couscous is well-prepared, topped with lots of nice veggies, and sweetened with raisins, cinnamon, and nuts. If the weather's good, sit outdoors and people-watch.

Inexpensive

burritoville

1489 First Ave. between 77th and 78th Sts. • 472–8800
141 Second Ave. between 8th and 9th Sts. • 260–3300
1606 Third Ave. between 90th and 91st Sts. • 410–2255
148 W. 4th St. near Sixth Ave. • 505–1212
451 Amsterdam Ave. between 81st and 82nd Sts. • 787–8181
36 Water St. near Broad St. • 747–1100
141 Second Ave. between 8th and 9th Sts. • 260–3300
144 Chambers St. near Hudson St. • 571–1144
70 W. 95th St. • 749–6534

The latest and greatest exciting installment in the continuing tale of the amazing, proliferating burrito parlor. Like many other of these establishments around town, Burritoville offers the delicious, reasonably priced, meal–for–a–day we've come to expect. The Lost In Austin Burrito has fresh spinach, mushrooms, brown rice, cheese, beans, pico de galo, and sour cream. We were able to substitute soy cheese and tofu sour cream for its Bovine derivatives with no problem ($1 extra, though). The Vegged Out in Santa Fe Burrito is totally vegan, and contains the usual stuff plus grilled vegetables. If you prefer a whole-wheat to a white flour tortilla, you've got to say so. Conclusion: pretty darn good. Incidentally, the Water St. location serves breakfast (including a great soy chorizo), and beer and wine are available.

Inexpensive

 1 4

cafe kapulsky

1217 Ave. J, near E. 13th St.
Midwood, Brooklyn • 718–338–3646
Hours: Sunday through Thursday 8 am to 11 pm; Friday 8 am to
one hour before Shabbat; Saturday one hour after Shabbat to
1:30 am

The U.S. franchise of what is apparently a vast network of
Cafes Kapulsky throughout the world. Kosher–dairy, tasty
food, friendly atmosphere. Plenty for lacto-ovo type folks, little for vegans. Everything is fresh and artfully prepared. Our
favorites are the fava bean plate (with humous) and the
potato latkes (pancakes). Try the melawah (a chewy,
doughy, savory fried thing—usually served with cheese and
a hard-boiled egg) or the bourekas with salad.

Moderate

cafe natural

2812 Ocean Ave. near Ave. X
Sheepshead Bay, Brooklyn • 718–648–4248
Hours: Sunday through Thursday 11 am to 10 pm; Friday and
Saturday 11 pm to 11 pm

Formerly Pizzarini Naturelle, Cafe Natural is a great place
to get whole-wheat pizza and salads as well as a number

of delicious, healthy entrees in southern Brooklyn. When last there, we had an appetizer of babaganoush (eggplant and tahini dip) served with hot whole-wheat pita bread, vegetarian chili over brown rice (excellent), stuffed eggplant rollatini (the stuffing in question being ricotta and mozzarella cheeses—*wunderbar*), and a vegetable pizza (prepared without cheese). There's a lovely glassed-in terrace, and the wait staff is helpful and friendly. Although they serve quite a bit of chicken, beef, and seafood, the offerings for vegetarians are fantastic.

Moderate

cafe viva

2578 Broadway near 97th St. • 663–VIVA; (800) 209–8482
Hours: Sunday through Thursday 11 am to 11:30 pm; Friday and Saturday 11 am to 11:30 pm

Vegetarian pizzeria and all around Italian restaurant supreme, Cafe Viva offers an unbelievable selection of pizzas made with a variety of vegetables and healthy gourmet ingredients. A few of the standouts for us are the whole-wheat pizza, the cornmeal pizza, the soy cheese pizza, and the incredible pesto pizza! And—we almost forgot — the Aztec pizza (grilled onions, sweet peppers, and corn) which is out of this world! If the pizzas aren't enough, they serve exceptional vegetarian lasagna, ravioli, and calzones, as well as a variety of salads, and there's a fresh juice bar. Drop everything and come here immediately!

Inexpensive

candle cafe

1307 Third Ave. near 75th St. • 472–0970
Hours: Monday through Saturday 7:30 am to 10:30 pm

Bart Potenza and Joy Pierson, co-owners of the Healthy Candle, one of the oldest and finest juice bars and natural food shacks in NYC have finally opened a restaurant—and it's fantastic! They seat 50 people and offer a wide selection of vegetarian, vegan, and macrobiotic goodies. Try the grilled tempeh portobello burger, or for a visual as well as a gastronomic treat, how about the "House of Paradise" casserole—a triplex of millet, black beans, and sweet potatoes built on a foundation of steamed kale. This hacienda of health overlooks a field of roasted vegetables and a pool of wild mushroom gravy. OK, so we spread the metaphor a little thin, but good housing is so hard to come by. Enjoy.

Moderate

caravan of dreams

405 E. 6th St. near First Ave. • 254–1613
Hours: Daily Noon to 11 pm

A cozy and friendly atmosphere combined with an exceptional and scrupulously prepared menu make a winning combination. The owner, Angel, is committed to the use of organic ingredients in all the dishes. When last there, we enjoyed the carbo platter (polenta with squash sauce and grain of the day) and the banana and carob shake made with almond milk, which was quite delish. Most of the food is dairy-free, and a good number of the dishes are wheat-free as well. They frequently have live music in the front and entertainment and various educational programs in the back room. Also, part of their receipts are donated to the "Green Corps," a training school for young environmentalists.

Moderate

chutney mary

40 E. 20th St. between Fifth and Madison Ave. • 473–8181
Hours: Monday through Friday 11:30 am to 3:30 pm and 5:30 pm to 11 pm; Saturday and Sunday 5:30 pm to 11 pm

Elegant and cozy Indian restaurant with the focus on dishes prepared with organically raised ingredients. They offer a large and delightful vegetarian/vegan menu including: The Raja's Jalfrezi (summer squash, sweet peppers, scallions, sprouts, eggplant and tomatoes in a light curry sauce), a wonderful dish entitled Ruby and Jade that includes red and green cabbage simmered with onions, tomatoes, coriander and herbs, and much more. They also serve seafood and chicken.

Expensive

commodities coffee bar

117 Hudson St. (Corner of N. Moore) • 334–8330
Hours: Monday through Saturday 8 am to 8 pm

Non–coffee drinkers should not be misled by the name of this place. Adjoining the extremely well-stocked Commodities Natural Food Supermarket, The Commodities Coffee Bar offers far more. They have a large selection of fresh juices and juice shakes, sandwiches like sunshine burgers, tempeh reubens, and unturkey, and like many coffee bars, it's a friendly place to sit and schmooze.

Inexpensive

dairy palace

2210 Victory Boulevard near Bradley Ave.

Staten Island • 718-761-5200

Hours: Sunday through Thursday 10:30 am to 8:30 pm; Friday 11 am to 2:30 pm; Saturday sundown to 12:30 am

Kosher dairy vegetarian restaurant and pizza joint with a deceptively humble exterior. They have a huge menu offering Middle Eastern delicacies such as "schwarma" and American staples like "steak" with fries, as well as an equally impressive Chinese menu offering such goodies as General Tso's "chicken" and pepper "steak." Most of the food is a little heavy on the grease, but we still felt very well-fed. A good place to visit if you're on Staten Island—however, don't expect either atmosphere or courtesy. The staff can be quite rude at times if you're not orthodox—or for that matter, even if you are.

Moderate

diamond dairy

4 W. 47th St. (2nd Floor, in the back) • 719-2694

Hours: Monday through Thursday 8 am to 5 pm; Friday 8 am to 2 pm; closed Saturday and Sunday

On 47th St., in the heart of the Diamond district, is the Jeweler's Exchange. Here you'll find a sort of flea market for ar-

20

ticles of adornment. In the back of the exchange, overlooking the stalls, is the real gem—the Diamond Dairy. Try the blintzes or the vegetable cutlet, both fantastic. A recurring special which is quite filling indeed is cholent with kugel. Cholent is Yiddish chili, and kugel is a baked pudding, most often made with either noodles (lukshen kugel) or potatoes.

Inexpensive

dining at rubi's

Mart 125 (260 W. 125th St.)
Mezzanine level, across from the Apollo Theater • 666–RUBI
Hours: Monday and Tuesday 10 am to 6:30 pm; Wednesday through Saturday 10 am to 7:30 pm; Sunday Noon to 5 pm

Directly across the street from the Apollo Theater is the Mart 125 Mall. Wind your way upstairs past a few stalls and there's Rubi's. Counter service with a couple of tables nearby. Plenty of vegetarian items, such as vegetarian burgers, veggie hot dogs, rainbow vegetarian special sandwich (in a pita), vegetarian "salmon," and "chicken" salad. The menu states: "For the best in tasty Afro–centric delicacies, health food for the body and soul." It's true. Catering is available, and organic produce is frequently used. For wheelchair access, use the elevator in the back.

Inexpensive

doctor squeeze

4 W. 23rd St. near Fifth Ave. • 243–5842

191 Columbus Ave. between 68th and 69th Sts. • 769–4848

Hours: Monday through Friday 8 am to 8 pm; Saturday and Sunday varies according to site.

If juicing is your thing, and compelling evidence suggests that it should be, check this place out. Juice bar (and *only* juice bar) extraordinaire. Everything squeezed on the spot, low prices, and quick service. Some specialties include the Big Squeeze (carrot, spinach, celery, and parsley); the wheatgrass "tooter"; the Atomic Squeeze (apples, sweet peppers, ginger, and parsley); and more. Hot, healthy soups in the winter.

Inexpensive

dojo restaurant

24 St. Mark's Pl. near Second Ave. • 674–9821

14 W. 4th St. near Mercer St. • 505–8934

Hours: Sunday through Thursday 11 am to 1 am; Friday and Saturday 11 am to 2 am

Bustling, new-age-style, pseudo–natural, quasi–Japanese bistros in the trendy East Village and the slightly less trendy area around New York University, where you can get a few notable vegetarian dishes. The Japanese brunch, served until 5 pm, comes with miso and a salad and includes steamed broccoli with tofu sauce over brown rice. Or for $2.95 you can get their famous soy burger platter (arguably the best veggie burger in New York), which comes with an ample portion of salad and a goodly helping of brown rice. Now that's a bargain!

Inexpensive

eden rock

2325 Broadway between 84th and 85th Sts. • 873–1361
Hours: Daily 9 am to Midnight

Lebanese restaurant on the Upper West Side. Veggies will find tabouli, babaganoush, lentils and rice, and the usual Middle Eastern fare. The quality is above average. Try the vegetable pie or the bamia (fried okra with tomatoes, onions, and Middle Eastern spices).

Inexpensive

eva's

11 W. 8th St. between Fifth and Sixth Aves. • 677-3496
Hours: Daily 10 am to 11:30 pm

Middle Eastern fast-food style restaurant with a broad selection of vegetarian salads and sandwiches (falafel, babaganoush, vine leaves with brown rice, baked tofu, and more). They also feature nature burgers (brown rice, sunflower seeds, herbs, spices) and veggie nuggets. Although they do serve some meat and fish dishes, the bulk of the menu is vegetarian and quite good. An ongoing deal here is that if you buy the special sandwich of the day, they give you another one for $1.50—not bad. In addition, there's a well-stocked natural foods store in the back.

Inexpensive

everything natural

3810 White Plains Rd. between 219th and 220th Sts.
Bronx • 718-652-9070
Hours: Monday through Saturday 8 am to 11 pm; Sunday 9 am to 9 pm

West Indian take-out restaurant with a good selection of hot vegetarian food sold by the plate, small for $4, medium for $6, and large for $8. You choose the size and tell them which goodies you want. Some options include vegetarian

24

"duck" with okra and white beans (delicious, but we believe it contains MSG), coconut rice and peas, and seasoned potatoes. They feature a fairly well-stocked natural foods store as well. Their menu states: "Jah annointeth our heads with oil, our blenders runneth over."

Inexpensive

everything vital

300 Troy Ave. (South of Eastern Parkway)
Crown Heights, Brooklyn • 718-953-9433
Hours: Daily 7:30 am to 10 pm

The Brooklyn branch of Everything Natural. Totally vegan, Caribbean, and delicious. This is a take-out place that our opinions diverge on, especially regarding one particular dish: the veggie "duck." It's made from curried tofu skins and comes with lima beans and sweet red peppers. One of us loves it, and one of us swears it contains MSG. The bulgur is great, and fresh juices are offered as well. The apple and carrot mixture is recommended. The sweet potato pudding will satisfy your sweet tooth, or for the ultimate sugar high, buy a piece of fresh sugar cane—chopped and peeled before your eyes.

Inexpensive

 25

famous pita

935 Coney Island Ave. bet. Ditmas and Newkirk Aves.
Kensington, Brooklyn • 718–282–0868
Hours: Monday through Thursday 8 am to 3 am; Friday 8 am to
4 pm; closed Saturday; Sunday 8 am to 3 pm

Israeli–Yemenite falafel joint supreme. Everything is made on
the premises, including the pita bread, which you can some-
times watch being baked in the back of the restaurant. A
sign says: "Hey, help yourself to our salad bar." This means
you can pile a $4 sandwich with as much of the salad
bar as you can fit—that's how it's done at falafel stands in
Israel. Don't miss the roasted eggplant at the end of the
bar. Also try the malawach, a chewy dough dish from
Yemen. Fresh hot soups are available, too—usually both
vegetable and bean. Make sure you sample the amba
sauce on your falafel. It's a tart, Iraqi–Indian specialty made
with a delicious mango base. Although some meat and
chicken dishes are sold, Famous Pita is the best example of
a "falafel with all–you–can–pile–on–salad–bar" emporium
in the Big Apple.

Inexpensive

freddie and pepper's gourmet pizzeria

303 Amsterdam Ave. between 74th and 75th Sts. • 799–BEST

Hours: Sunday through Thursday 11 am to 11:30 pm; Friday and Saturday 11 am to 3 am

Deceptively standard–looking pizzeria with a couple of quite notable exceptions: you can get just about any vegetable as a topping, and they have whole–wheat pizza and freshly baked soy cheese pizza. The cheese used on this is a product called Soya melt, which the owners say is totally without dairy. We have our suspicions, but that's what they say. The decor and ambiance are easily as seedy as many another NYC pizzerias, but would you rather have the pristine, ketchup–covered cardboard of a Pizza Hut?

Inexpensive

good food cafe (now: healthy lunch)

401 Fifth Ave. near 38th St. • 686–3546

Hours: Monday through Friday 11:30 am to 7 pm; Saturday Noon to 5 pm; closed Sunday

Located a few blocks from the Empire State Building, this place is a find. Service is cafeteria–style (serve yourself) and there's a friendly and comfortable seating area. They have a great selection, reasonable prices, and portions are generous. The tofu–mushroom casserole with brown rice and sprouts is fantastic. Although some fish and chicken dishes are sold, they have a large, well–prepared vegetarian menu. Specials change daily. Have a late dinner here and then go watch the sunset from the E.S.B. observatory.

Inexpensive

good health cafe

324 E. 86th St. between First and Second Aves. • 439–9680
Hours: Monday through Thursday 11:30 am to 10 pm; Friday
11:30 am to 11 pm; Saturday and Sunday 10 am to 10 pm

We ordered the whole–wheat dumplings served with an array of steamed vegetables and tamari ginger sauce, which made for a light, exquisite meal. A companion had the macro plate that included hijiki, black–eyed peas (which were the bean of the day), brown rice, and steamed vegetables. The desserts are good—our blueberry–peach pie, for example, was super. Like its companion restaurants Quantum Leap and Village Natural, there are always daily specials and a casserole of the day. Also, there's a well–stocked natural foods store on the premises for your grocery–shopping pleasure.

Moderate

gourmet cafe

1622 Coney Island Ave. between Aves. L and M
Midwood, Brooklyn • 718–338–5825
Hours: Monday through Thursday 11:30 am to 10 pm; closed
Friday and Saturday; Sunday 12:30 pm to 10 pm

Kosher, vegetarian dairy restaurant/cafe in the heart of Midwood providing high–quality vittles to the community. Plenty
of meat substitutes are available, such as vegetarian Hun-
garian goulash, Bombay "chicken," and a delicious soy
schnitzel. They also have some very nice frozen meals to
take home and a line of delicious muffins. Monday through
Thursday, dinner entrees are half price. A bargain!

Moderate

govinda's

In front of 80 Broadway near Wall St.
Hours: Seasonally, Monday through Friday 11 am to 3 pm

Cute little pushcart located in front of 80 Broadway at the
corner of Wall St. (a mere stone's throw from the Stock Exchange), sporting an awning festooned with pictures of various Hindu deities. Try the veggie burger, which is served in
a pita and is fantastic (especially for the price), the vegetarian chili, or soup. Freshly squeezed juices are available as
well, along with various seasonal treats.

Inexpensive

29

great american health bar

2 Park Ave. between 32nd and 33rd Sts. • 685–7117
Hours: Monday through Wednesday 7 am to 7 pm; Thursday 7 am
to 8 pm; Friday 7 am to 3 pm; closed Saturday and Sunday
35 W. 57th St. between Fifth and Sixth Aves. • 355–5177
Hours: Daily 8 am to 10 pm
821 Third Ave. near 50th St. • 758–0883
Hours: Monday through Friday 7:30 am to 8 pm; Saturday and
Sunday 11 am to 8 pm

These places are great! Styled after 1940s lunch counters,
they're a vegetarian's answer to McDonald's. Soup, sandwiches, salads and fresh juices—all natural, mostly vegetarian. All three sites are kosher and except for the one on W.
57th St., wheelchair–accessible.

Moderate

gulliver's living and learning center–liliput cafe

120 W. 41st St. between Sixth Ave. and Broadway • 730–LIFE
Hours: Monday through Friday 11 am to 2:30 pm; closed Saturday
and Sunday

Cozy little vegan cafe and take–out in the heart of midtown,
run under the aegis of the very wonderful Gulliver's Living
and Learning Center. They have an unbelievable and varied

30

menu that changes daily, offering such delectable treats as tempeh scallopini, tofu lasagna, seitan fajitas and much, much more. The quality of food here is exceptional! They also have a general store offering some natural groceries and a line of non–leather footwear. Who knows, once you're here, maybe you'll stay for a class or lecture. One speaker of note was the late Benjamin Spock. Ya gotta love this place!

Inexpensive

hangawi

12 E. 32nd St. between Fifth and Madison Aves. • 213–0077
Hours: Monday through Saturday 11 am to 11 pm; Sunday 11 am to 10:30 pm

Traditional Korean vegan cuisine in the neighborhood currently known as Little Korea. They have a number of full–course meals (which they don't allow you to share), such as the supreme vegetarian meal, which includes porridge, eight different kinds of side dishes, seven kinds of greens, mini–pancakes, a deep–fried vegetable and mushroom assortment, bean paste soup, and dessert. You'll have an elegant, unique, and delectable dining experience, but for an unbelievable amount of money.

Expensive

health pub

371 Second Ave. near 21st St. • 529–9200
Hours: Daily 11 am to 11 pm; kitchen closes at 10:30 pm

Upscale, nearly vegan restaurant in Gramercy Park (none of the food is made with meat, eggs, dairy products, or sugar—however, they do serve fish) with an extremely high-quality menu. Some available goodies are marinated grilled tofu, golden corn bread with amaranth, Oriental stir–fry, and black bean chili. The seitan marsala with brown rice and kale is superb, and the almond pudding with cherry sauce was the best thing we've had in years. They also serve organic wines. You've never really had good wine until you've had some made from unsprayed grapes and without chemical additives. The hazelnut carob torte with raspberry topping is exquisite, too.

Expensive

healthy chelsea

248 W. 23rd St. near Eighth Ave. • 691–0286
Hours: Monday through Saturday 10 am to 10 pm; Sunday Noon to 9 pm
Take–out health food store and juice bar with a small vegetarian steam table. By the end of the day some of the entrees

32

in their steam table look a bit ragged, so go early for the best quality. Some sandwiches and shakes are available as well.

Inexpensive

healthy henrrieta's

60 Henry St. between Cranberry and Orange Sts.,
Brooklyn Heights, Brooklyn • 718–858–8478

healthy henrrieta's on the slope

787 Union St. near Sixth Ave.
Park Slope, Brooklyn • 718–622–2924
Hours: Daily 11 am to 11 pm

Wonderful, high–quality, vegetarian, macrobiotic Mexican restaurants. You can have either regular or tofu sour cream on your burrito and a choice of black, pinto, or aduki beans and yellow or brown rice. They use organic beans and grains and filtered water, and everything on the menu is *muy delicioso*. The Park Slope branch has the same basic menu—macrobiotic Mexican—and decor as the flagship branch in Brooklyn Heights. Brilliant choice of location, this is a half a block from the Park Slope Food Coop.

Inexpensive

healthy pleasures

93 University Pl. near 11th St. • 353–FOOD

Hours: Daily 7 am to 10 pm

One of the newest and finest natural food supermarkets. Besides a huge selection of healthy groceries, they offer a sumptuous salad bar, and a delicious and bountiful natural deli take–out section, with goodies such as sauteed seitan and curried tempeh.

Inexpensive–Expensive

helianthus

48 MacDougal St. near King St. • 598–0387

Hours: Monday through Saturday 11 am to 11 pm; Sunday Noon to 11 pm

"Helianthus," which our ancient Roman readers will know means "sunflower," has successful sister restaurants in both Taipei and Tokyo. The decor here in New York is light and airy with pictures of sunflowers everywhere. The food is delicious. Try the veggie "pork" with vegetables (carrots, green peppers, and pineapple in a sweet and sour sauce) or the veggie "steak" with black pepper sauce. We started with an appetizer of yako tofu, which is a platter of cold silky bean curd topped with minced "ham," mushrooms, and a mildly hot ginger tamari sauce—incredible! We followed with one of the best versions of General Tso's "chicken" we've ever had. Sherman, the owner of Helianthus, is both conscientious and committed to excellence. Try the box lunches, too. They're a bargain.

Moderate–Expensive

hong kong vegetarian

1400 Second Ave. between 72nd and 73rd Sts. • 472–8717 or 472–8749

Hours: Monday through Saturday Noon to 11 pm; Sunday and Holidays 1 pm to 11 pm

A relatively new kid on the block, Hong Kong Vegetarian is a welcome addition to the Upper East Side. It's vegetarian Chinese, if you couldn't guess. Totally vegan, good selection. Try the stir–fried rainbow "eel" or the "scallops" Szechuan–style. Affiliated with the renowned House of Vegetarian restaurant in Chinatown.

Moderate–Expensive

 3 5

house of falafel vegetarian style

620 Nostrand Ave. between Dean and Pacific Sts.
Bedford–Stuyvesant, Brooklyn • 718–735–0009
Hours: Monday through Saturday 11 am to 8:30 pm; closed
Sunday

Very nice take–out place with a little counter. They have a different menu for every day of the week. The macaroni pie comes "en casserole" and is stuffed with veggies. Delicious. The callaloo (a green vegetable similar to spinach) is served creamed with coconut and West Indian spices. And of course, the falafel with the "works" (which, as one might imagine, is their specialty) is simply great.

Inexpensive

house of vegetarian

68 Mott St. between Canal and Bayard Sts. • 226–6572
Hours: Daily 11 am to 11 pm

Vegetarian Chinese restaurant on Chinatown's main street, offering very good fare at quite reasonable prices. We especially like the lemon "chicken" and the iron "steak" (both made from white yams). The mock "ham" is seasoned just right. For your appetizer, try the assorted gluten and/or the gluten "duck" (they're both delicious) or the spring rolls, which are a bit greasy. But who knows, maybe you like that.

Moderate–Expensive

hunan delight

752 Union St. near Sixth Ave.
Park Slope, Brooklyn • 718–789–1400/1415
Hours: Monday through Thursday 11:30 am to 10:30 pm; Friday and Saturday 11:30 am to 11:30 pm; Sunday 1 pm to 10:30 pm

The menu says: "In accordance with traditional Buddhist/vegan practice, all our dishes are prepared entirely with vegetables and vegetable derivatives." Egg whites, however, are used in some dishes, and there's a separate menu for meat eaters. The corn and fresh mushroom soup, which is thick and sort of like a porridge, is great. The steamed vegetable dumplings are a little bland, but the steamed spinach dumplings are delicious. The spicy sesame "chicken" is amazing (if a bit on the sweet side), and the taro "chicken" a la king (with fresh vegetables, a crispy taro root crust, and a savory sauce) is extraordinary.

Moderate

indian delhi

392 Columbus Ave. near 79th St. • 362–8760

Hours: Monday through Saturday 11 am to 11 pm; Sunday 11 am to 11 pm

This used to be the Indian Kitchen (on 78th and Broadway), which was too wonderful for words. Then the all–too–common "landlord problems" intervened and they had to move. Like its former incarnation, they serve great vegetarian Indian food in an inspirational and peaceful setting. Try the "Indian falafel" (chick–peas, cabbage, and salad wrapped up in a flat pita topped with onion relish)—a bargain—or get a vegetable combo plate with your choice of any three veggies over rice (another bargain, especially considering the quality). We are sad to note, though, that this long–standing strictly vegetarian establishment has begun serving chicken and fish! We hope that by the next edition of this book they will have reconsidered.

Inexpensive

integral yoga

299 W. 13th St. between Seventh and Eighth Aves. • 243–2642
Hours: Monday through Friday 10 am to 9:30 pm; Saturday 10 am
to 8:30 pm; Sunday Noon to 6:30 pm

Extremely well-stocked natural food store with a little something extra in the back. That "something extra" is one of the
best take-out salad bars and steam tables in the city. Items
from the steam table include tofu ravioli, bok choy and tofu,
and lemon tempeh, and more. Among the sandwiches they
offer are their "faloney" sandwich and mock tuna. They also
offer wonderful vegetarian cooking classes, available
through their bookstore next door. Integral Yoga has been in
the 14th St. area providing natural food to New Yorkers for
at least 20 years. We applaud their efforts.

Inexpensive

i rankin' ital stop

804 Nostrand Ave. between St. John's and Lincoln Pls.
Crown Heights, Brooklyn • 718–467–7630
Hours: Monday through Saturday 9 am to 10 pm; closed Sunday

All praise to His Majesty Haile Selassie I. The food here is
strictly "Ital," which means "no flesh is served." The veggie

patty has a gram burger filling (gram burger is a West Indian meat substitute, sort of like textured vegetable protein or soy grits, the texture similar to ground beef) in a coconut–like dough—it's delicious. There are a few tables and a long counter; you get your food from the counter and sit down or take it out. Fresh breads and cakes are available as well.

Inexpensive

josephina

1900 Broadway near Lincoln Center • 799–1000
Hours: Monday through Friday Noon to Midnight; Saturday 11:30 am to Midnight; Sunday 11:30 am to Midnight

Sophisticated, upscale, natural food restaurant in a roomy, comfortable, well–decorated space, offering a delectable and healthy menu, including quite a bit for vegans and vegetarians. Organically raised produce is frequently used, and most of the entrees are dairy–free. Everything here is a treat for the taste buds. Try the protein plate (quinoa, wheat berries, and a vegetable tortilla). Fills in the gap around Lincoln Center. If you're eating here before the theater, reservations are suggested; otherwise just mosey on in with lots of cash.

Expensive

josie's

300 Amsterdam Ave. near 74th St. • 769-1212
Hours: Sunday through Thursday 5 pm to 10:30 pm; Friday and
Saturday 5 pm to Midnight

Like that of its sister restaurant Josephina, the *raison d' etre*
here is to provide high–quality, well–prepared, natural cuisine, and thus change your mind about how good natural
food can be. We'll drink to that! While their commitment to
meatless cuisine is commendable, Josie's is also a viable op-
tion for a mixed (veggie and carnie) group, as they offer
many of the American standards as well–albeit healthily
prepared.

Moderate

kar

5908 Ave. N near Ralph Ave.
Mill Basin, Brooklyn • 718-531-8811
Hours: Monday through Thursday Noon to 10:30 pm; Friday and
Saturday Noon to 11:30 pm; closed Sunday
2212 Ave. X between E. 22nd and E. 23rd Sts.,
Sheepshead Bay, Brooklyn • 718-891-6868 (take-out only)
Hours: Monday through Thursday 11:30 am to 10 pm; Friday and
Saturday 1 pm to 11:30 pm; closed Sunday

 41

Superb Chinese restaurants with an emphasis on low salt, low fat, fresh, healthy food. Brown rice is available, and they don't use MSG, either. Service is always exceptional, and the food always superb. The interesting thing about Kar is that they have different specials at each branch. Try the whole–wheat vegetable dumplings for an appetizer, or the baby eggplant with garlic sauce. The crispy tofu pot is scrumptious.

Moderate

kar luk

437 Fifth Ave. near 9th St.
Park Slope, Brooklyn • 718–832–4500
Hours: Monday through Thursday 11:30 am to 10:30 pm; Friday and Saturday 11:30 am to 11:30 pm; Sunday 12:30 pm to 10:30 pm

To all outward appearances, your standard Chinese take–out with a few tables. However, Kar–Luck (run by the former first chef of the now closed Kar of Park Slope) is a wonderful, health–oriented Chinese restaurant on Fifth Ave. that offers an extensive vegetarian menu, and the vegetarian sesame chicken in particular is excellent. The vegetarian hot and sour soup is a little too salty for our taste.

Inexpensive

knish nosh

101–02 Queens Boulevard near 67th Rd.
Forest Hills, Queens • 718–897–5554
Hours: Monday and Saturday 9 am to 7 pm; Tuesday through
Friday 9 am to 7:30 pm; Sunday 9 am to 6 pm

A longtime Forest Hills mainstay, this fine kosher knishery
serves no meat, of course (consistent with kosher law), and
offers such mouth–watering goodies as fresh spinach, broccoli, kasha, and carrot knishes as well as the more familiar
potato ones, all made on the premises.

Inexpensive

kosher corner

73–01 Main St. near 73rd Ave.
Kew Garden Hills, Queens • 718–263–1177
Hours: Sunday through Thursday 7:30 am to 10 pm; Friday 7:30
am to 2 pm; closed Saturday

Kosher dairy sit–down restaurant in the orthodox Jewish
community located around Main St. and Jewel Ave. Their
vegetable cutlet with mushroom sauce is very good, as is the
French onion soup. They have a children's menu as well.

Moderate

le poeme

14 Prince St. near Elizabeth St. • 941–1106

Hours: Daily 8:30 am to 11 pm

Friendly, laid–back, Corsican restaurant in the area com-
prising the juncture of Little Italy, SoHo, and the Lower East
Side. All the food is reasonably priced and fresher than
fresh. We started with the three–dip plat du jour, the dips in
question being eggplant, humous, and tapenade (black
olives and garlic—ooh la, la!), served with the most wonderful homemade whole–wheat bread (which can be taken
home for $4 a loaf— it's worth it). The vegetable lasagna
was supposedly vegan (it had no visible signs of cheese or
eggs, but our suspicion lingers). Nevertheless, it was delicious.

Moderate

lenox ave.
health food restaurant

471 Lenox Ave. (A.K.A. Malcolm X Blvd) between 133rd and
134th Sts. • 368–7663

Hours: Monday through Saturday 7 am to 8 pm

Rastafarian vegetarian restaurant. Lunch specials, served
from 11 am to 3 pm, allow you to choose any three items
for $5, or you can get any two items with the vegetarian
lasagna, which is fantastic. Try the vegetarian "scallops" or

the callaloo. They have an incredible selection for breakfast as well—the scrambled tofu with a side of plantains is particularly good. Menus change daily. On your way over, check out the African bazaar on Lenox Ave. between 125th and 128th Sts.

Inexpensive

life cafe

343 E. 10th St. near Ave. B • 477–9001

One Sheridan Square near W. 4th St. • 929–7344

Hours: Monday through Thursday Noon to Midnight; Friday Noon to 2 am; Saturday 11 am to 2 am; Sunday 11 am to Midnight

Artsy little cafes with lots and lots of vegan and vegetarian items, such as the mega burrito (made with seitan), the seitan steak sandwich (meatless version of the "Philly steak sandwich"), a whole bunch of soy drinks, and much more. The original establishment in the East Village began as a "performance space" that took its name from the old Life magazine covers the owners put in the windows to cover up the holes. Either branch is a great place to hang out with friends, drink coffee or beer, have a bite, and debate the nature of the universe.

Moderate

liveth's delight vegetarian restaurant

1358 St. John's Pl.

Weeksville, Brooklyn • 718–735–4008

Hours: Monday through Saturday 11:30 am to 9:30 pm; closed Sunday

Vegetarian take–out counter/restaurant near Weeksville (one of the oldest African–American neighborhoods in NYC). When we were there the lo–mein was good and fresh, but the mixed vegetables were not. However, the bean dishes we sampled, made variously with cow peas, chick–peas or red peas were quite delicious, and the macaroni pie and gran burgers were great.

Inexpensive

lucky's juice joint

75 W. Houston St. near W. Broadway • 388–0300

Hours: Monday through Saturday 9 am to 8 pm; Sunday 10 am to 8 pm

Friendly little place at the northern border of ultrachic SoHo. Lucky's is structured mostly for take–out, however; they have a small amount of counter space and give the impression of a down–home shack, particularly in the context of the surrounding architecture. They offer a plethora of sandwiches, healthy desserts and of course a fine selection of juices. Spend a couple of hours in the SoHo galleries, then come to Lucky's for some rejuvenating refreshments.

Inexpensive

madras mahal

104 Lexington Ave. between 27th and 28th Sts. • 684–4010
Hours: Daily 11:30 am to 3 pm; 5 pm to 10 pm

Exceptional kosher Indian vegetarian restaurant on the site of what was once the justifiably renowned Madras Palace. We feel that the quality and variety of food far surpasses that of the former occupant. Unlike many other vegetarian Indian places, they offer vegetarian dishes from all over India, not just from the Southern provinces. The mixed vegetable uthappam (a pancake made of rice and lentil flour) is delicious. So is the masala dosai, which resembles a gigantic crepe. In all, you can have a sumptuous repast here worthy of the Vedic gods.

Moderate

 47

mana

2444 Broadway between 90th and 91st Sts. • 787–1110

Hours: Monday through Saturday 11:30 am to 11 pm; Sunday Noon to 10 pm

This is the site of the original Souen's, which was quite a hit when it opened. Mana has the same delicious cuisine, and the same high standards (no sugar, chemicals, or dairy products), turning out quality, Japanese–style, macrobiotic food at fairly reasonable prices. They do serve fish, however. Try the seitan sukiyaki, it's wonderful.

Moderate

matamim kosher dairy restaurant

5001 13th Ave. near 50th St.

Boro Park, Brooklyn • (800) 303–2522

Hours: Sunday through Thursday 9 am to 9 pm; Friday 9 am to 2 pm; closed Saturday

Kosher Dairy restaurant formerly known as Taam Eden (A Taste of Eden) in the heart of Boro Park. Blintzes, latkes, stuffed cabbage (veggie–style, natch), vegetarian chopped "liver," and kugels, plus all the dishes you would expect, and all very well–prepared. As a matter of fact, the quality here is exceptional. Take–out is available, and you have the choice of dining in either their informal coffee–shop type area in the front, or the schmaltzy Catskills–style dining room in the rear. Don't miss trying the cholent (meatless Yiddish chili that will really stick to your ribs).

Moderate in the front
Expensive in the back

mathilda's bakery, m...m...m... (a.k.a. roger's famous muffins)

1321 Ave J at E. 14th St.
Midwood, Brooklyn • 718-951-8148
Sunday through Thursday 7 am to 8 pm; Friday 7 am through sundown; closed Saturday

A kosher dairy bakery and catering, and yes, those "M"s are part of the restaurant's name. Very nice people. Delicious baked goods all made on the premises, including borekas (an Israeli staple—phylo dough triangles filled with spinach, potato, or cheese) and a huge assortment of cakes, cookies, and other goodies, many of which are made with little or no salt or sugar. You can get babaganoush or a number of other salads on a bagel or on a platter, and they also make special holiday items like Hanukkah jelly doughnuts and latkes. Their pride and joy, however, are their muffins.

Inexpensive

mavali palace

46 E. 29th St. between Park and Madison Aves. • 679–5535
Hours: Tuesday through Sunday Noon to 10 pm; closed Monday

South Indian vegetarian restaurant extraordinaire! Enter and you're in an ancient Hindu temple. You're immediately seduced by the scents of incense and cardamom, and the beautiful and fascinating statuary of deities all around the room (many in delightful states of undress). The staff is helpful, friendly and eager to please. Needless to say this is a splendid place for a date or anniversary celebration. There are certain restaurants where you know that highly conscientious, passionate artists are at work in the kitchen— Mavali Palace is one. Omitting the dairy products in any dish is not a problem, so they're definitely vegan–friendly. The chick–pea masala is exquisite, as is the idly, and the menu goes on and on. Many feel that this is among the best Indian food available in NYC. We heartily agree.

Moderate

melanie's natural cafe

445 Sixth Ave. near 10th St. • 463-7744

Hours: Monday through Friday 8 am to 10 pm; Saturday 9 am to 10 pm; Sunday 11 am to 10 pm

Again that word—"Natural!" What does it mean? Close to the earth? Back to the land? No pesticides or preservatives? What? Melanie's is a cafeteria–style place in the heart of the West Village. As for the food, there are quite a few salads and vegetarian entrees. The Cajun, spiced tofu salad with brown rice and veggies is pretty good. The staff, though courteous and helpful, is a bit unaware regarding the dietary needs of vegans. Go there and make them change that. While you're there, seat yourself by the window looking onto Sixth Ave. and people–watch.

Inexpensive

michael & zoë's (formerly brownie points)

101 Second Ave. between 5th and 6th Sts. • 254-5004

Hours: Sunday through Thursday 8 am to 11 pm; Friday and Saturday 8 am to 1 pm

Snappy little spot that specializes, as the former name implies, in homemade brownies (many of which are natural and vegan). They also have a very nice menu offering quite

51

a few vegetarian entrees. In the sandwich department, for example, they have vegetarian chicken salad, sunshine burgers, and veggie burgers. They have a very good vegetarian cashew chili too. Try "Lorraine's Own," which is a mixture of brown rice, wild rice, and assorted vegetables. And don't forget the brownie.

Moderate

mr. falafel

226 Seventh Ave. between 3rd and 4th Sts.
Park Slope, Brooklyn • 718–768–4961
Hours: Daily 11 am to 10:30 pm

Congenial Egyptian restaurant and take–out in Park Slope serving many of the choices you might expect from Middle Eastern cuisine. The food is prepared with great care, and special attention is given to providing quite a few choices for their vegetarian clientele. Falafel, babaganoush, humous, foul moodamas (fava beans with lemon juice, garlic, and olive oil), Egyptian potato salad, and more. Stop in and say hello to the Missus. Incidentally, the owner's name is Aladdin, and he will grant your every culinary wish.

Inexpensive

 5 2

mrs. stahl's knishes

1001 Brighton Beach Ave. (Entrance on Coney Island Ave.)
Brighton Beach, Brooklyn • 718–648–0210
Hours: Daily 9 am to 7 pm

A million and one knishes. Well, perhaps we're exaggerating a bit. You've probably had a potato knish, maybe even a kasha knish somewhere along the line, but have you ever had a cabbage, sweet potato, potato and mushroom, or Spanish rice knish? The list goes on like you wouldn't believe and everything is made by hand. Get a dozen assorted, walk two blocks to the ocean, and enjoy. And yes, Virginia, there once was a Mrs. Stahl, who started out by peddling knishes on the boardwalk during the Depression.

Inexpensive

natural food bar

166 W. 72nd St. between Broadway and Amsterdam Ave. •
874–1213
Hours: Monday through Saturday 8 am to Midnight; Sunday Noon to 10 pm

Teeny–tiny, itsy–bitsy, claustrophobic little place with a big, big, superbig menu. They have sandwiches (the vegetarian

5 3

chicken salad is delicious), salads, soups, juices, and more.
They make vegetarian egg rolls, veggie patties, and a vegetarian "cheeseburger" that's fantastic. The homemade
cakes are great too.

Inexpensive

nature works

200A W. 44th St. between Broadway and Eighth Ave. •
869–8335
Hours: Monday through Saturday 10 am to 9 pm; closed Sunday

Snappy little joint in the heart of the Theater District serving
Middle Easternesque cuisine that leans toward the healthy,
including salads, veggie burgers, falafels, soups, and more.
Tasty, high–quality morsels with a respectable ratio of bite
for the buck. Great location. It's good to know that after
you've dropped $200 on *Les Miz* or *Miss Saigon* (ooh, a
real helicopter!) you can still get something to eat with what's
left in your pocket.

Inexpensive

nyota's ting

718–217–0583
Days: Whenever and wherever they pop up
Call for a schedule, home delivery, or catering.

Wonderful, totally vegan African–American food service that provides catering and home delivery. Our favorite dish has always been the barbecued gluten "ribs," but they have a couple of dozen other great offerings as well. Some stand-outs are the tofu orange "duck," and the soy "sausage" pepper and onion plate (a veggie version of those insidious meat things so common at street fairs). They also sell their wares at street fairs, often showing up at the New Life fair in Manhattan.

Inexpensive

oasis

137 Seventh Ave. near Carroll St.
Park Slope, Brooklyn • 718–783–0215
Hours: Sunday through Thursday 11 am to 10:30 pm; Friday and Saturday 11 am to 11:30 pm

Middle Eastern cuisine. Our ilk may dine here with impunity since they serve falafel, humous, babaganoush, omelets, and salads. If you don't do dairy, you have to make a point of telling them or they'll assume otherwise (we ordered

5 5

grape leaves, which automatically came covered with yogurt). We found the servings to be a bit skimpy and the prices a bit high. If you're looking for high–quality food at a reasonable price, this place is less an oasis than a mirage.

Moderate

OZU

566 Amsterdam Ave. near 87th St. • 787–8316
Hours: Sunday through Thursday Noon to 10 pm; Friday and Saturday Noon to 11 pm

Austere, macrobiotic Japanese restaurant on the Upper West Side with a somewhat regular crowd and a very high–quality menu. Some of the goodies we enjoyed were the mabo tofu (stir–fried tofu with ground seitan, broccoli, and fungi in a black bean sauce) and the ozu croquette (couscous, millet, kasha, and lentils), which comes with a choice of tofu, seitan, or beet sauce and is served with a green salad. Our daughter enjoyed the soba mariko, which is noodles sauteed with vegetables in tomato–miso sauce and served with a deep–fried seitan cutlet. She claimed that "it almost tasted like spaghetti." If you suffer from tofu–phobia, please come here. They serve 50,000 kinds of tofu prepared 60,000 different ways. Well, perhaps we're stretching the

 **5 6**

truth just a bit. However, the selection is quite broad. Desserts are well-prepared and include many non-dairy, sugar-free yummies such as the almond creme caramel. Like many macrobiotic restaurants, they also serve fish.

Moderate-Expensive

planet one

76 E. 7th St. near First Ave. • 475-0112
Hours: Daily Noon to Midnight

The atmosphere at Planet One is warm and friendly, and the prices are low. When we last ate here, the soup of the day, a red lentil with squash, was delicious, and reminded us of a thick curried dahl. The roti, a whole wheat Jamaican bread filled with curried vegetable stew, red cabbage, zucchini, and carrots, was super. The vegetable plate is also a good deal. We had the collard greens, West African rice, and African okra cooked with garlic, tomatoes, and spinach. A companion who usually hates okra loved this. The owners of Planet One, Maima and Annette, are very nice, and only too happy to cater to most folks' diets. Primarily vegetarian, but some seafood and free-range chicken is served.

Inexpensive

plum tree

1501 First Ave. between 78th and 79th Sts. • 734–1412
Hours: Tuesday through Sunday Noon to 10 pm; closed Monday

Macrobiotic cuisine with an emphasis on the food of Asia.
Try the soy corn bread or Woman Warrior Stew (tofu, seitan, veggies, and burdock). Brunch is also available from
Noon to 4 pm on Saturdays and Sundays, with such wonderful choices as buckwheat pancakes or scrambled tofu. A
great place to have a relaxing, healthy meal.

Moderate

quantum leap

65–64 Fresh Meadow Lane
Fresh Meadows, Queens • 718–461–1307
88 W. 3rd St. between Thompson and Sullivan Sts. • 677–8050
Hours: Monday through Thursday 11 am to 10:45 pm; Friday and
Saturday 11 am to 11:45 pm; Sunday 11 am to 10 pm

Longtime mainstay for vegetarians in New York. They serve
casseroles, salads, soups, and tempura, as well as a weekend brunch including whole–grain pancakes and waffles.
Try the daily specials. The Mexican Fiesta is good, and so
is the seitan parmigiana. The miso soup is hearty with lots of

 58

vegetables. Sample the sweet potato tempura as well and don't forget a slice of tofu pie for dessert. The original branch in Queens, which has a well–stocked natural–foods store next door, is in a tree–lined neighborhood that, for New York, is positively bucolic.

Moderate

ratner's dairy restaurant

138 Delancey St. between Norfolk and Suffolk Sts. • 677–5588
Hours: Sunday through Thursday 6 am to 10:30 pm; Friday 6 am to 3 pm; closed Saturday

Oy, such food! Kosher dairy restaurant supreme. The three "B"s: blintzes, bagels, and borscht (and that's just for appetizers). Lots of kosher fish dishes, too. Ratner's offers a huge, well–prepared menu, and is the home of the wise–guy waiters in the old–time, kosher–restaurant tradition. Bring lots of dough, though–you're eating in a tourist attraction. Hey, maybe afterward you could go shopping on Orchard St. and find a bargain. Actually, the days of bargains on Orchard St. are long gone—try Chambers St. a few blocks south.

Expensive

red hot szechuan

347 Seventh Ave. at 10th St.
Park Slope, Brooklyn • 718–369–0700/0702
Hours: Monday through Thursday 11 am to 10:30 pm; Friday and
Saturday 11:30 am to 11 pm; Sunday 12:30 pm to 10:30 pm

Vegetarian Chinese food has come to Brooklyn, and the
quality is pretty high. The Sauteed veggie "pork" with bar-
becue sauce is scrumptious—served with snow peas, onions
and a "fish" carved out of a zucchini as a garnish. The
sweet and sour "ribs" are great and the hot and sour soup
is excellent.

Moderate–Expensive

salad bowl

Pier 17, South St. Seaport • 693–0590
901 Sixth Ave., Manhattan Mall • 594–6512
566 Seventh Ave. near 41st St. • 921–7060
Hours: Daily 7 am to 9 pm (varies according to site; call first)

All–natural–food restaurants featuring on–premises cooking
and baking. Quite a lot for vegans and vegetarians. To wit:
vegetable cheese casserole, vegetable lasagna, vegetarian
chili, eggplant parmigiana, veggie burgers, and of course,

lots and lots of salads. The list is long. Don't miss their scrumptious desserts; we're partial to the cranberry bread ourselves.

Inexpensive

salad daze

390 Whitehall Street at the NY Health and Racquet Club, near Water and State Sts. • 509–0077

Hours: Monday through Friday 7:30 am to 6 pm; closed Saturday and Sunday

Cafeteria–style (you line up and order, then bring it to your table) salad place with a high–quality selection that includes a good number of meatless salads. One of our favorites is the Salad Daze Specialty (romaine, plum tomatoes, red peppers, mushrooms, cucumbers, red onions, and avocado pesto). They also have a large number of delicious pasta dishes. Quality is always high, and prices are quite reasonable.

Inexpensive

sanctuary

33 St. Marks Pl. (8th St.) between Second and Third Aves. •
505–8234

Hours: Tuesday through Saturday Noon to 8:30 pm; closed Sunday
and Monday

The Sanctuary is primarily an interfaith spiritual center offering symposia and lectures on a wide variety of religious topics. However, if your aim is nothing more than a gratifying discourse between your stomach, tongue, and wallet, they have a vegetarian buffet that is both good and cheap. Check this out: $5—we said *$5*—for all you can eat! The offerings are mostly vegan and primarily Indian or Middle Eastern. Check out the vegetarian chili (T.V.P. and tofu) if they have it.

Inexpensive

smile of the beyond

86–14 Parsons Boulevard near Hillside Ave.
Jamaica, Queens • 718–739–7453
Hours: Monday through Friday 7 am to 4 pm; Saturday 7 am to
3 pm; closed Sunday

Vegetarian luncheonette that serves breakfast and lunch and is affiliated with Sri Chinmoy and the Annam Brahma restaurant nearby. The place has a beautiful sky–blue decor and

62

an old–fashioned soda machine with vintage 70s logos. The waiters are disciples of Sri Chinmoy, and the quality of the food is pretty high. Try the "turkey" club sandwich, the soy "steak" burger, or the vegetarian "B.L.T."—all meatless. The chocolate cake with vanilla icing is quite sweet. Cool name for a restaurant, don't you think?

Inexpensive

souen

28 E. 13th St. between University Pl. and Fifth Ave. • 627–7150
210 Sixth Ave. near Prince St. • 807–7421
Hours: Monday through Friday 10 am to 10 pm; Saturday and Sunday 10 am to 11 pm

Macrobiotic restaurant supreme. If you can't find it here, you're in bad shape, pal. No meat, eggs, or dairy, although they do serve fish, and they try to get organic produce when they can. Try the seitan cutlets, tempeh croquettes, and noodles with kuzu sauce (carrot and burdock), or just have a bowl of the best miso soup in New York. Have you ever had seitan sushi? Good stuff for breakfast too—like mochi waffles, even with fakin' bacon. "Souen," by the way, means "green garden" in Japanese.

Moderate

spring street natural

62 Spring St. (Entrance on Lafayette St.) • 966–0290

Hours: Sunday through Thursday 11:30 am to Midnight; Friday and Saturday 11:30 am to 1 am

Quality restaurant in SoHo providing elegantly prepared dishes using a preponderance of organically raised ingredients. Although they serve fish, chicken, and dairy, they have quite a good selection for vegetarians and vegans. Try the tempeh burger or the semolina fettuccine with shiitake mushrooms. The corn–fried seitan with dipping sauce is also delicious.

Moderate

steve & sons bakery, restaurant & caterers

9305 Church Ave. near E. 93rd St.

Brownsville, Brooklyn • 718–498–6800

Hours: Monday through Thursday 7 am to Midnight; Friday 7 am to 6 pm; Saturday 6 pm to Midnight; Sunday 7:30 am to Noon

Wonderful West Indian (Grenadian) restaurant–bakery in Brownsville. Steve & Sons prepares many vegetarian dishes using wheat gluten. A particular favorite of ours is the vegetarian barbecued "ribs." All the entrees are served with rice and peas. This is the "home of the vegetarian patties"—their meatless version of the West Indian staple, made with soy protein and a whole–wheat crust (if you specifically ask for whole wheat). Their freshly made desserts are fantastic, and we never go home without a loaf of "hot from the oven" whole–wheat bread.

Inexpensive

strictly roots

2058 Adam Clayton Powell Blvd. between 122nd and 123rd Sts.
• 864–8699
Hours: Daily 9 am to 10:30 pm

A sign on the wall states that Strictly Roots "serves nothing that crawls, walks, swims, or flies." Totally vegan Rastafarian restaurant and take–out. You ask for the platter size you want: small for $4.50, medium for $7, large for $9, then choose the foods to go in it. The rice and peas and the veggie duck were both delicious.

Inexpensive

taqueria

72 Seventh Ave. between Berkeley and Lincoln Pl.

Park Slope, Brooklyn • 718–398–4300

341 Seventh Ave. between 9th and 10th Sts.

Park Slope, Brooklyn • 718–624–7498

8 Bergen St. near Court St.

Cobble Hill, Brooklyn • 718–624–7498

355 Sixth Ave. (Manhattan) near Waverly Pl. • 229–0999

Hours: Daily Noon to 11 pm (some variance according to location)

"Authentic" East L.A. Mexican Food—very good, hearty "stick to your ribs" fare. The vegetarian burrito for $6.25 is a meal for the day. Quality is quite high. Try the vegetarian taco or the San Juaquin burrito (all vegetarian), or just get some rice and beans. Although they do use a lot of sour cream and cheese in many of the dishes, you can request that your food be prepared without dairy and they'll gladly comply. Who knows—perhaps the day will come when we'll see a taqueria on every street corner in America.

Moderate

temple in the village

74 W. 3rd St. between LaGuardia Pl. and Thompson Sts. • 475–5670

Hours: Monday through Saturday 11 am to 10 pm; closed Sunday

Small, buffet–style natural–food cafeteria with a great selection of delicious veggies, noodles, and grains. In other words, an extensive natural, vegetarian salad bar with a couple of tables where you can sit and chow down after you've piled up your plate and paid. If the weather's nice, get yourself a helping to go, walk a block to Washington Square Park, and listen to some Bob Dylan wanna–be.

Inexpensive

teva natural foods

122 E. 42nd St. near Lexington Ave. • 599–1265
Hours: Monday through Friday 7 am to 5 pm; closed Saturday and Sunday

Kosher dairy Middle Eastern spot serving falafel, babaganoush, vegetarian chopped liver, vegetable cutlets, and more. They're on the concourse level of the Chanin building (downstairs) on your way to the subway. Nice people, good food. Right near Grand Central Station. Primarily take–out, but they also have a couple of stools and a counter.

Inexpensive

topaz

127 W. 56th St. between Sixth and Seventh Aves. • 957–8020
Hours: Monday through Thursday 11 am to 11 pm; Friday 11 am to
4:30 pm; Saturday 4 pm to 11:30 pm; Sunday 4 pm to 11 pm

High–quality Thai restaurant with a good number of vegetarian entrees, many of which are vegan and all of which
are beautifully prepared (some with rose petals). Some recommended choices are the vegetarian duck, the vegetables
and pepper in coconut milk curry, and the delicious gang
som pak soup (which is made with corn, cabbage, and Thai
herbs).

Moderate–Expensive

uptown juice bar
(and vegetarian deli)

60 W. 125th St. between Fifth and Lenox Aves. • 987–1188
Hours: Monday through Saturday 9 am to 8 pm; closed Sunday

In the heart of Harlem, the Uptown Juice Bar is mostly for
take–out, but they do have a couple of chairs if you want to
wolf something down. They offer veggie sandwiches (Ital
"chicken," "beef," and "turkey"), veggie burgers, salads,
and, of course, a wide selection of juices. They also do
catering.

Inexpensive

6 8

vegetable garden

15 E. 40th St. between Fifth and Madison Aves. • 545–7444
Hours: Monday through Thursday 7 am to 9 pm; Friday 7 am to
3 pm; closed Saturday and Sunday

Formerly an outpost of The Great American Health Bar, this
place is swell. It boasts a large, very clean dining area and
a spiffy–looking counter up–front if you're rushed. Now to
the food. The salads are fresh and healthy. They have a
bunch of soups that you can get with extras like brown rice,
a muffin, or a salad, as well as a bevy of baked potatoes,
stuffed with the likes of vegetarian chili or steamed vegetables. While there is an emphasis on fish and dairy (it being
a kosher dairy restaurant and all), lots of other goodies are
available as well. The hot vegetable cutlet sandwich is very
good and they have no problem whatsoever with your request to hold the cheese that normally tops it. It is served
quickly and elegantly with a salad and a side of french fries.
They also have some nice entrees like vegetable lasagna,
Oriental vegetables over brown rice, and specials which
change daily. Breakfasts are pretty standard fare (eggs and
fries), with a few notable exceptions—you can get a bowl
of granola or some piping hot oatmeal served with honey,
as well as a variety of freshly squeezed juices.

Inexpensive

vege vege ii

544 Third Ave. between 36th and 37th Sts. • 679–4710/4702
Hours: Daily 11:30 am to 11 pm

Wonderful, elegant, friendly, certified kosher, positively scrumptious, totally vegetarian Asian restaurant. The founder, Mama Pang, was formerly the chef at Zen Palate, and the food, in quality and artistry of presentation, reflects the standard of that restaurant without being as snooty. The entire staff is gracious and extremely solicitous of their customers' comfort. For appetizers, try the moo shu basil rolls (marvelous, filled with nuts and wrapped in basil) or the barbecued, grilled satay (made from gluten). As for the main course, the selection is so broad that you may find it difficult to decide. The curried vegetarian "chicken" is quite good and almost indistinguishable from a hearty stew, and the "chicken" a la king is superb. We recently had a veggie "lamb" made from formosan mushrooms that was unbelievable. They also serve beer and wine. This is an excellent place to bring potential "converts."

Moderate

vegetarian delights (and meat dishes)

3604 Clarendon Rd. near E. 36th St.

Flatbush, Brooklyn • 718–284–9605

Hours: Monday through Saturday 9 am to Midnight; closed Sunday

Take–out joint serving both Rastafarian–style vegetarian and West Indian meat dishes. Among the many vegetarian specialties are Jamaican veggie patties, vegetable roti (pretty good), tofu dinner (spicy fried tofu with veggies), Ital stew (various vegetables, rice and peas, salad, and whatnot). Ackee (a West Indian nut–like fruit) and vegetables make a nice combination. Desserts include sweet potato pudding, cornmeal pudding, and carrot cake. Breakfast is also available.

Inexpensive

vegetarian garden

37 E. 29th St. between Park and Madison Aves.• 686–9691

Hours: Daily 11 am to 11 pm

Vegetarian Chinese restaurant in the Buddhist tradition offering a huge selection including quite a few meat substitute dishes like vegetarian "pork" chops with lemon sauce, sliced "beef" with broccoli and sweet and sour "ribs." They also have a good number of plain ol' vegetable dishes like snow cabbage and fresh mushrooms casserole. The lunch specials are available from 11 am to 3:30 pm and give you a very good bite for the buck.

Inexpensive–Moderate

vegetarian heaven

304 W. 58th St. (4 Columbus Circle) near Eighth Ave. •
956–4678
Hours: Sunday through Thursday 11 am to 11 pm; Friday 11 am to sundown; closed Saturday

This sister restaurant of Bamboo Garden in Flushing is an excellent kosher, vegetarian Chinese restaurant with a huge and delectable menu. They're located on Columbus Circle, which is a short walk to the Theater District and Times Square. Try one of the many varieties of "chicken" or "beef" or the barbecued "ribs." The best bets cost–wise are the lunch specials—a heapin' helpin' of vittles for an extremely reasonable price.

Moderate–Expensive

 7 2

vegetarian paradise 2 (vp2)

144 W. 4th St. near Sixth Ave. • 260–7130

vp2 go

140 W. 4th St., also near Sixth Ave.

Hours: Sunday through Tuesday and Thursday 11:30 am to 9:30 pm; closed Wednesday; Friday and Saturday 11:30 am to 10:30 pm

Progeny of the justly famous Vegetarian Paradise in Chinatown, VP2 is simply a more elegant, expensive version of the original downtown location. The portions are a little smaller than at the original, but the food is just as wonderful. You'll have a very good dining experience here, and the Village location is great, but try VP3 on Mott St. for the best value. VP2 GO, as one might expect, is for take–out, and offers an excellent selection of vegan, macrobiotic dim sum.

Expensive

vegetarian paradise 3

33–35 Mott St. • 406–6988/2896

Hours: Sunday through Thursday 11 am to 10 pm; Friday and Saturday 11 am to 11 pm

VP returns to Chinatown! Millions cheer! Many of you may know of VP only through VP2 or VP2–GO in the Village.

However, the original Vegetarian Paradise was the first Vegetarian Chinese restaurant in New York. It was located on the Bowery near Canal St. in Chinatown, and closed a few years ago due to structural damage in the building. VP3 boasts a clean, roomy, well–designed space that is also wheelchair–accessible, as well as the yummy, mouth–watering food that made them famous.

Moderate

village natural

46 Greenwich Ave. between Sixth and Seventh Aves. • 727–0968
Hours: Monday through Thursday 11 am to 11 pm; Friday 11 am to Midnight; Saturday and Sunday 11 am to 10 pm

Excellent, moderately priced vegetarian restaurant in the West Village. We enjoyed the seitan parmigiana (excellent), the soba (buckwheat noodles) with tahini (super), and the tostada platter with everything (beans, cheese, guacamole, sour cream), which was filling and satisfying. We also had the millet croquetts, which came with brown rice, aduki beans, steamed veggies, and a tamari ginger sauce. The ambiance is friendly and pleasant, and the service is excellent. Good tofu pies, too—sweetened with maple syrup.

Moderate

weiss' kosher dairy restaurant

1146 Coney Island Ave. near Ave. H
Midwood, Brooklyn • 718–421–0184
Hours: Sunday through Thursday Noon to 10 pm; Friday Noon to a
few hours before sundown; closed Saturday until 90 minutes after
sundown

Pursuant to kosher edicts, dairy restaurants permit absolutely
no meat or meat products on the premises (if you don't count
fish). Some specialties here include blintzes (cheese, potato,
blueberry), kasha varnishkas (buckwheat groats with bowtie
noodles), vegetable "steak" with mushroom sauce, and a
pretty good vegetarian Shepherd's Pie. Quality is high. Atmosphere is Catskills to the gills. They have a $10 per plate
minimum no matter what you select, so beware! Hey, Monday night is all you can eat—bring the family and friends.

Expensive

west indian vegetarian and seafood restaurant

752 Nostrand Ave. between Park and Sterling
Crown Heights, Brooklyn • 718–778–7100
Hours: Daily 8 am to 8:30 pm

Dinky little take–out joint frequently permeated with the smell
of fresh herbs. The chicklet stew is made with Worthington's

canned meat substitutes (which we believe has MSG), but we still think it tastes pretty good. The macaroni and cheese is great, as is the stir-fried cabbage, and of course the rice and peas.

Inexpensive

whole earth bakery and kitchen

70 Spring St. between Broadway and Lafayette St. (SoHo) • 226–8280

130 St. Mark's Pl. near Ave. A (East Village) • 677–7597

Hours: Monday through Saturday 8 am to 9 pm; Sunday 10 am to 8 pm

A bakery *and* kitchen—whole–earthwise, that is. Sumptuous take–out stores. They make delicious natural baked goods, such as cakes, cookies, and muffins, most of which contain no sugar, honey, or dairy products and are strictly vegan. They also have assorted extras like raisin bun sandwiches, cheese biscuits, whole–wheat poppyseed crackers, tofu veggie rolls, cabbage or black bean turnovers, made–to–order cakes, and juices galore. Their motto is: "Simple food for complex times." 'Nuf said.

Moderate

whole foods in soho

117 Prince St. between Greene and Wooster Sts. • 673–5388
Hours: Daily 9 am to 9:30 pm

Strictly take–out natural foods market/deli that is definitely
worth knowing about if you're in the area and need a little
nosh to tide you over. They have a huge and wonderful
salad bar and an incredible steam table with plenty of vegetarian selections. The market is fairly well–stocked with natural foods.

Moderate

who's on seventh?

183 Seventh Ave. near 1st St.
Park Slope, Brooklyn • 718–965–0597
Hours: Daily 11 am to 11 pm; Saturday and Sunday brunch 11 am
to 4 pm

"Natural"–style restaurant, which claims to make everything
from scratch. Weekend brunches are served with fresh fruit,
and include whole–grain pancakes or vegetable omelets.
The yellow corn enchilada is OK and the tofu sunflower
burger we found to be only so–so. Non–dairy dishes are
available as well. Park Slope–style prices. Bottom line,
though: Even though the management is blasé and the over-
all quality is bland, bland, bland, they are natural, vegetar-

7 7

ian, and centrally located to serve the Park Slope community. *Caveat emptor.*

Moderate–Expensive

yonah shimmel's

137 E. Houston St. between First and Second Aves. • 477–2858
Hours: Daily 8 am to 7 pm

You haven't had a knish until you've been here. All kinds of knishes, and handmade, too. Kasha, cheese, potato, ad infinitum. It's not kosher, but it's been here about 100 years or so, and there's good reason. Try the 100–year–old yogurt—don't worry, it was in the fridge—we mean the culture for the yogurt is 100 years old…oh, you know what we mean.

Inexpensive

zen palate

633 9th Ave. at 46th St. • 582–1669
34 Union Square East near 16th St. • 614–9345
Hours: Monday through Friday 11:30 pm to 10:45 pm; Saturday 11 am to 11 pm; Sunday Noon to 10:30 pm

Vegetarian Oriental "bistro" on restaurant row (W. 46th St.) and somewhat recently on Union Square as well. Snooty and expensive, but the food is good. (They had a great guiding force at their inception—see Vege Vege II). The hot and sour vegetable soup we had was excellent, as were the vegetable dumplings. For an entree, the "sweet and sour divine" (deep–fried pecan puffs with peppers in a sweet and sour sauce) was delish and the sunset on pagoda (taro root rolls with almonds) was super. Regarding their branch near Union Square—downstairs: cheap and friendly; upstairs: the service is snooty as ever. Nonetheless, we still heartily recommend it, as the food is delicious and the setting in both locations is elegant.

Inexpensive-Expensive

glossary

Gluten: A complex of protein from cereal grains which, with the addition of water, becomes elastic and has a characteristic texture. Gluten enhances the rising of bread with the help of leavening.

Macrobiotic: The application of specific ancient oriental philosophies to diet. The concepts of yin and yang are applied to the alkaline and acid qualities in foods, with the goal of having a neutral pH diet. Local foods are encouraged, and are often prepared in Japanese or Japanese-style cuisine.

Miso: A fermented soybean paste made from soybeans, miso starter, salt, and occasionally rice or barley. It can be diluted with broth and eaten as a soup or added undiluted to many foods as a seasoning.

Rennet: A dried extract of the stomach lining of calves, lambs, kids, or pigs used in the curdling of milk for cheese–making. Some cheeses, however, may use vegetable rennet.

Seitan: Wheat gluten separated from the other components of wheat and cooked in soy sauce. Its characteristic flavor and texture are somewhat akin to that of meat. Seitan is frequently used in many dishes as a meat substitute.

Tempeh: A fermented soybean product native to Indonesia. The soybeans are inoculated with a culture called rhizopus, which is grown on hibiscus leaves, and which provides it with both a high B vitamin content and a distinctive flavor. Tempeh can be prepared in a number of ways, and is often mixed with grains and vegetables.

Tofu: Soybean curd, or—to be more exact—cheese made from soy milk. A food quite high in protein and native to many Asian cultures. Tofu comes in different textures such as soft or firm and so can be used in many different ways. Soft tofu is best for custards or puddings, whereas firm tofu is preferable for stir–fry or recipes where you need it to hold together. Tofu is somewhat bland by itself, but delicious when seasoned.

Vegan: One who excludes all animal products, such as meat, fish, fowl, eggs, dairy products, and honey from their diet. Many vegans also eschew the use of animal products in other areas of their life as well, such as clothing made from leather or wool.

Vegetarian: One who avoids animal products in a more loosely and variably defined manner than your average vegan. Many vegetarians include eggs and milk, and some include fish in their diets.

index by neighborhood

DOWNTOWN/WALL ST.
American Cafe   **4**
Burritoville   **14**
Govinda's   **29**
Healthy Henrrieta's   **33**
Ratner's Dairy Restaurant   **59**
Salad Bowl   **60**

TRIBECA
Commodities Coffee Bar   **19**

CHINATOWN
House of Vegetarian   36
Hunan Delight   37
Vegetarian Paradise 3   73

SOHO
Abyssinia   3
Bell Cafe   11
Helianthus   34
Le Poeme   44
Lucky's Juice Joint   46
Souen   63
Spring Street Natural   64
Whole Earth Bakery and Kitchen   76
Whole Foods in SoHo   77

EAST VILLAGE
Angelica Kitchen   6
B & H Dairy   9
Benny's Burritos   12
Burritoville   14
Caravan of Dreams   18
Dojo Restaurant   22
Life Cafe   45
Michael & Zoë's   51
Planet One   57

86

Sanctuary   **62**
Whole Earth Bakery and Kitchen   **76**
Yonah Shimmel's   **78**

WEST VILLAGE
Benny's Burritos   **12**
Integral Yoga   **39**

CENTRAL VILLAGE
Apple Restaurant   **8**
Boostan   **13**
Burritoville   **14**
Dojo Restaurant   **22**
Eva's   **24**
Healthy Pleasures   **34**
Melanie's Natural Cafe   **51**
Quantum Leap   **58**
Red Hot Szechuan   **60**
Souen   **63**
Taqueria   **66**
Temple in the Village   **66**
Vegetarian Paradise 2/
 VP 2 GO   **93**
Village Natural   **74**

GRAMERCY PARK/UNION SQUARE

Health Pub   32
Zen Palate   78
Chutney Mary   18
Zen Palate   78

CHELSEA

Bachué   9
Doctor Squeeze   22
Healthy Chelsea   32

EAST MIDTOWN

Blanche's Organic Cafe   12
Good Food Cafe   27
Great American Health Bar   30
Hangawi   31
Madras Mahal   47
Mavali Palace   50
Teva Natural Foods   67
Vege Vege II   70
Vegetable Garden   69
Vegetarian Garden   71

WEST MIDTOWN

Diamond Dairy   20

Great American Health Bar 30
Gulliver's Living and Learning Center 30
Nature Works 54
Salad Bowl 60
Topaz 68
Zen Palate 78

UPPER EAST SIDE
Blanche's Organic Cafe 12
Burritoville 14
Candle Cafe 17
Good Health Cafe 28
Hong Kong Vegetarian 35
Lenox Ave. Health Food Restaurant 44
Plum Tree 58

UPPER WEST SIDE
Burritoville 14
Cafe Viva 16
Dining at Rubi's 21
Doctor Squeeze 22
Eden Rock 23
Freddie and Pepper's
  Gourmet Pizzeria 27
Indian Delhi 38
Josephina 40

Josie's   41
Lenox Ave. Health Food Restaurant   44
Mana   48
Natural Food Bar   53
Ozu   56
Strictly Roots   65
Uptown Juice Bar   68
Vegetarian Heaven   72

BROOKLYN
Cafe Kapulsky   15
Cafe Natural   15
Everything Vital   25
Famous Pita   26
Gourmet Cafe   29
Healthy Henrrieta's   33
House of Falafel Vegetarian Style   36
Hunan Delight   37
I Rankin' Ital Stop   39
Kar   41
Kar Luk   42
Liveth's Delight Vegetarian Restaurant   46
Matamim Kosher Dairy Restaurant   48
Mathilda's Bakery, M...M...M...   49
Mr. Falafel   52
Mrs. Stahl's Knishes   53
Nyota's Ting   55

Oasis   55
Red Hot Szechuan   60
Steve & Sons Bakery, Restaurant   64
Taqueria   66
Vegetarian Delights (And Meat Dishes)   71
Weiss' Kosher Dairy Restaurant   75
West Indian Vegetarian and Seafood   75
Who's on Seventh?   77

QUEENS
Anand Bhavan   4
Annam Brahma   4
Bamboo Garden Restaurant   10
Knish Nosh   43
Kosher Corner   43
Quantum Leap   58
Smile of the Beyond   62

BRONX
Everything Natural   24

STATEN ISLAND
Dairy Palace   20

index by cuisine

AFRICAN–AMERICAN
Dining at Rubi's   21
Nyota's Ting   55

AFRICAN
Abyssinia   3

COFFEE AND JUICE BARS
Commodities Coffee Bar   19
Doctor Squeeze   22

93

**Uptown Juice Bar and
Vegetarian Deli   68**

CHINESE
Bamboo Garden Restaurant   10
Hong Kong Vegetarian   35
House of Vegetarian   36
Hunan Delight   37
Kar   41
Kar Luk   42
Red Hot Szechuan   60
Vegetarian Garden   71
Vegetarian Heaven   72
Vegetarian Paradise   73

COLUMBIAN
Bachué   9

CORSICAN
Le Poeme   44

ECLECTIC
Apple Restaurant   8
Bell Cafe   11

Blanche's Organic Cafe   12
Cafe Natural   15
Candle Cafe   17
Caravan of Dreams   18
Dojo   22
Good Food Cafe   27
Good Health Cafe   28
Great American Health Bar   30
Health Pub   32
Healthy Chelsea   32
Healthy Pleasures   34
Integral Yoga   39
Josephina   40
Josie's   41
Life Cafe   45
Liveth's Delight Vegetarian Restaurant   46
Lucky's Juice Joint   46
Melanie's Natural Cafe   51
Michael & Zoë's   51
Natural Food Bar   53
Nature Works   54
Planet One   57
Quantum Leap   58
Salad Bowl   60
Salad Daze   61
Sanctuary   62
Smile of the Beyond   62
Spring Street Natural   64

9 5

Temple in the Village   66
Vegetable Garden   69
Village Natural   74
Who's on Seventh?   77
Whole Earth Bakery and Kitchen   76
Whole Foods in SoHo   77

INDIAN

Anand Bhavan   4
Annam Brahma   7
Chutney Mary   18
Govinda's   29
Indian Delhi   38
Madras Mahal   47
Mavali Palace   50

ITALIAN

Cafe Viva   16
Freddie and Pepper's Gourmet Pizzeria   27

KNISHERIES

Kinish Nosh   43
Mrs. Stahl's Knishes   53
Yonah Shimmel's   78

KOSHER

American Cafe   4
B & H Dairy   9
Cafe Kapulsky   15
Dairy Palace   20
Diamond Dairy   20
Gourmet Cafe   29
Kosher Corner   43
Matamim Kosher Dairy Restaurant   48
Mathilda's Bakery, M...M...M...   49
Ratner's Dairy Restaurant   59
Teva Natural Foods   67
Vegetarian Heaven   72
Weiss' Kosher Dairy Restaurant   75

KOREAN

Hangawi   31

MACROBIOTIC

Mana   48
Ozu   56
Plum Tree   58
Souen   63

MIDDLE EASTERN

Boostan   **13**
Eden Rock   **23**
Eva's   **24**
Famous Pita   **26**
House of Falafel   **36**
Mr. Falafel   **52**
Oasis   **55**
Teva Natural Foods   **67**

MEXICAN

Benny's Burritos   **12**
Burritoville   **14**
Healthy Henrrieta's   **33**
Taqueria   **66**

PAN-ASIAN

Helianthus   **34**
Vege Vege II   **70**
Zen Palate   **78**

THAI

Topaz   **68**

9 8

VEGAN

Angelica Kitchen   6
Gulliver's Living and Learning Center—
    Liliput Cafe   30
Nyota's Ting   55
Strictly Roots   65

WEST INDIAN

Everything Natural   24
Everything Vital   25
I Rankin' Ital Stop   39
Lenox Ave. Health Food Restaurant   44
Steve & Sons Bakery, Caterers &
  Restaurant   64
Strictly Roots   65
Vegetarian Delights   71
West Indian Vegetarian
  and Seafood Restaurant   75

Critical Acclaim for

Vegetarian Dining in New York City Third and Fourth Editions

"The first guide of its kind, 'Vegetarian Dining in New York City . . .', includes not only straight out vegetarian eateries, but regular restaurants that have a substantial number of vegetarian dishes on the menu, Kosher dairy restaurants, and restaurants serving ethnic cuisines in which vegetarian cooking features heavily." **—New York Newsday**

"All vegetarians, along with their health–conscious omnivorous friends, should find something good to eat in 'Vegetarian Dining in New York City'."

—New York Daily News

"'Vegetarian Dining in New York City . . . ' Lists vegetarian/vegan restaurants in all five boroughs . . . extensive"

—Vegetarian Journal

"Top of the class"

—N.Y. Magazine

about the authors

Arthur Brown is a former cab driver, a stand–up comic, native New Yorker, and evangelical vegetarian. **Barbara Holmes** holds a degree in nutrition from Brooklyn College and works for a Brooklyn W.I.C. program. She follows a plant–centered diet. They are married and have a daughter, Jasmine.

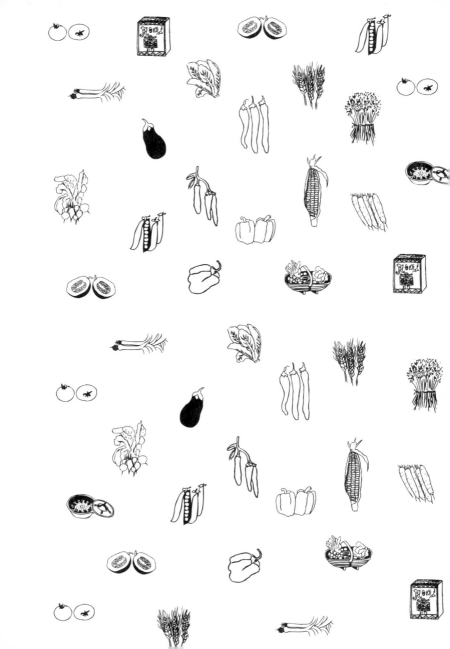

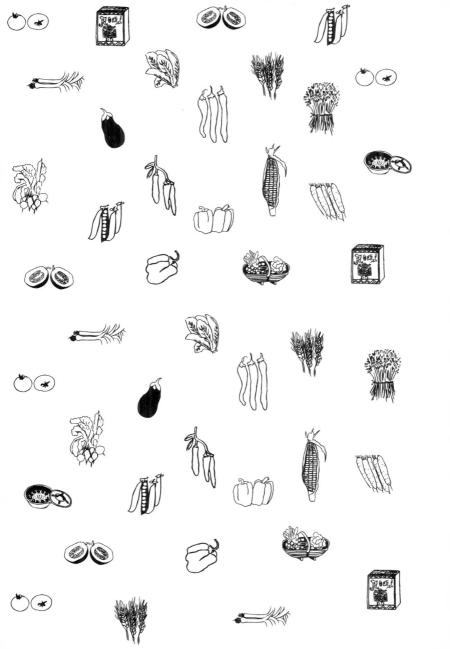

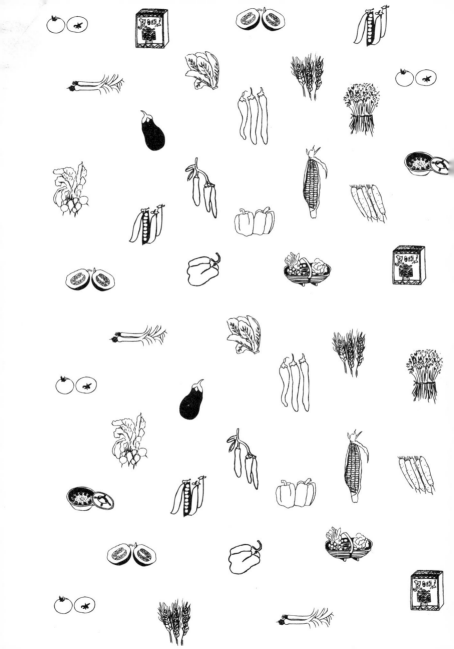